# The Lions Book of
# Young Verse

D1390554

*Other Young Lions Poetry Books*

The Song that Sings the Bird    *ed. Ruth Craft*
Salford Road and other poems    *Gareth Owen*
Song of the City    *Gareth Owen*
Mind Your Own Business    *Michael Rosen*
When Did You Last Wash Your Feet?    *Michael Rosen*
Hairy Tales and Nursery Crimes    *Michael Rosen*
Out of the Blue    *Fiona Waters*
A Children's Zoo    *ed. Julia Watson*
Rabbiting On    *Kit Wright*

The Lions
Book of

# YOUNG VERSE

chosen by
Julia Watson
and illustrated by
Quentin Blake

Young Lions
*An Imprint of HarperCollinsPublishers*

First published in Young Lions 1973
Fourteenth impression February 1993

Young Lions is an imprint of
HarperCollins Children's Books,
a division of HarperCollins Publishers Ltd,
77–85 Fulham Palace Road,
Hammersmith, London W6 8JB

This collection © Julia Watson 1973
Illustrations © Quentin Blake 1973

The author asserts the moral right to be
identified as the author of the work

Printed and bound in Great Britain by
HarperCollins Manufacturing, Glasgow

Conditions of Sale
This book is sold subject to the condition
that it shall not, by way of trade or otherwise,
be lent, re-sold, hired out or otherwise circulated
without the publisher's prior consent in any form of
binding or cover other than that in which it is
published and without a similar condition
including this condition being imposed
on the subsequent purchaser.

# CONTENTS

5

# Animals and Strange Creatures

## DOWN THE STREAM
## THE SWANS ALL GLIDE

Down the stream the swans all glide;
It's quite the cheapest way to ride.
Their legs get wet,
Their tummies wetter:
I think after all
The bus is better.

*Spike Milligan*

# SEAL

See how he dives
  From the rocks with a zoom!
  See how he darts
    Through his watery room
    Past crabs and eels
      And green seaweed,
      Past fluffs of sandy
      Minnow feed!
    See how he swims
      With a swerve and a twist,
  A flip of the flipper,
  A flick of the wrist!
Quicksilver-quick,
Softer than spray,
Down he plunges
And sweeps away;
Before you can think,
Before you can utter
Words like 'Dill pickle'
Or 'Apple butter',
  Back up he swims
    Past sting-ray and shark,
    Out with a zoom,
    A whoop, a bark;
      Before you can say
      Whatever you wish,
        He plops at your side
        With a mouthful of fish!
                        *William Jay Smith*

8

## AN INTRODUCTION TO DOGS

The dog is man's best friend.
He has a tail on one end.
Up in front he has teeth.
And four legs underneath.

Dogs like to bark.
They like it best after dark.
They not only frighten prowlers away
But also hold the sandman at bay.

A dog that is indoors
To be let out implores.
You let him out and what then?
He wants back in again.

Dogs display reluctance and wrath
If you try to give them a bath.
They bury bones in hideaways
And half the time they trot sideways.

They cheer up people who are frowning,
And rescue people who are drowning,
They also track mud on beds,
And chew people's clothes to shreds.

Dogs in the country have fun.
They run and run and run.
But in the city this species
Is dragged around on leashes.

Dogs are upright as a steeple
And much more loyal than people.
Well people may be reprehensibler
But I still think they are sensibler,
Because as Mr Benchley found,
They can lie down without turning
    three times around.

*Ogden Nash*

# THE SONG OF THE WHALE

Wouldn't you like to be a whale
And sail serenely by –
An eighty-foot whale from the tip of your tail
And a tiny, briny eye?
Wouldn't you like to wallow
Where nobody says 'Come out!'
Wouldn't you *love* to swallow
And blow all the brine about?
Wouldn't you like to be always clean
But never have to wash, I mean,
And wouldn't you love to spout –
O yes, just think –
A feather of spray as you sail away,
And rise and sink and rise and sink,
And blow all the brine about?

*Geoffrey Dearmer*

## ALGY MET A BEAR

Algy met a bear,
A bear met Algy.
The bear was bulgy,
The bulge was Algy.

*Anon*

## SKIMBLESHANKS: THE RAILWAY CAT

There's a whisper down the line at 11.39
When the Night Mail's ready to depart,
Saying 'Skimble where is Skimble has he gone to hunt
    the thimble?
We must find him or the train can't start.'
All the guards and all the porters and the station-
    master's daughters
They are searching high and low,
Saying 'Skimble where is Skimble for unless he's very
    nimble
Then the Night Mail just can't go.'
At 11.42 then the signal's overdue
And the passengers are frantic to a man –
Then Skimble will appear and he'll saunter to the rear:
He's been busy in the luggage van!
    He gives one flash of his glass-green eyes
        And the signal goes 'All Clear!'
    And we're off at last for the northern part
        Of the Northern Hemisphere!

You may say that by and large it is Skimble who's in
   charge
Of the Sleeping Car Express.
From the driver and the guards to the bagmen playing
   cards
He will supervise them all, more or less.
Down the corridor he paces and examines all the faces
Of the travellers in the First and in the Third;
He establishes control by a regular patrol
And he'd know at once if anything occurred.

He will watch you without winking and he sees what
   you are thinking
And it's certain that he doesn't approve
Of hilarity and riot, so the folk are very quiet
When Skimble is about and on the move.
   You can play no pranks with Skimbleshanks!
      He's a Cat that cannot be ignored;
   So nothing goes wrong on the Northern Mail
      When Skimbleshanks is aboard.

Oh it's very pleasant when you have found your little
   den
With your name written up on the door.
And the berth is very neat with a newly folded sheet
And there's not a speck of dust on the floor.
There is every sort of light – you can make it dark or
   bright:
There's a button that you turn to make a breeze.
There's a funny little basin you're supposed to wash
   your face in
And a crank to shut the window if you sneeze.

15

Then the guard looks in politely and will ask you very
	brightly
'Do you like your morning tea weak or strong?'
But Skimble's just behind him and was ready to
	remind him,
For Skimble won't let anything go wrong.
	And when you creep into your cosy berth
		And pull up the counterpane,
	You ought to reflect that it's very nice
	To know that you won't be bothered by mice –
	You can leave all that to the Railway Cat,
		The Cat of the Railway Train!

In the watches of the night he is always fresh and
	bright;
Every now and then he has a cup of tea
With perhaps a drop of Scotch-while he's keeping on
	the watch,
Only stopping here and there to catch a flea.
You were fast asleep at Crewe and so you never knew
That he was walking up and down the station;
You were sleeping all the while he was busy at Carlisle,
Where he greets the stationmaster with elation.
But you saw him at Dumfries, where he summons the
	police
If there's anything they ought to know about:
When you get to Gallowgate there you do not have to
	wait –
For Skimbleshanks will help you to get out!
	He gives you a wave of his long brown tail
		Which says: 'I'll see you again!
	You'll meet without fail on the Midnight Mail
		The Cat of the Railway Train.'

T. S. Eliot

# ANT AND ELEPH-ANT

Said a tiny Ant
To the Elephant,
'Mind how you tread in this clearing!'

But alas! Cruel fate!
She was crushed by the weight
Of an Elephant, hard of hearing.

*Spike Milligan*

## ENIGMA SARTORIAL

Consider the Penguin.
He's smart as can be –
Dressed in his dinner clothes
Permanently.
You never can tell,
When you see him about,
If he's just coming in
Or just going out!

*Lucy W. Rhu*

## I KNEW A BLACK BEETLE

I knew a black beetle, who lived down a drain,
And friendly he was, though his manners were plain;
When I took a bath he would come up the pipe,
And together we'd wash and together we'd wipe.

Though mother would sometimes protest with a sneer
That my choice of a tub-mate was wanton and queer,
A nicer companion I never have seen;
He bathed every night, so he must have been clean.

Whenever he heard the tap splash in the tub
He'd dash up the drain-pipe and wait for a scrub,
And often, so fond of ablution was he,
I'd find him there floating and waiting for me.

But nurse has done something that seems a great
     shame:
She saw him there, waiting, prepared for a game:
She turned on the hot and she scalded him sore
And he'll never come bathing with me any more.

*Christopher Morley*

# THE FOUR FRIENDS

Ernest was an elephant, a great big fellow,
    Leonard was a lion with a six-foot tail,
George was a goat, and his beard was yellow,
    And James was a very small snail.

Leonard had a stall, and a great big strong one,
    Ernest had a manger, and its walls were thick,
George found a pen, but I think it was the wrong one,
    And James sat down on a brick.

Ernest started trumpeting, and cracked his manger,
    Leonard started roaring, and shivered his stall,
James gave the huffle of a snail in danger
    And nobody heard him at all.

Ernest started trumpeting and raised such a rumpus,
  Leonard started roaring and trying to kick,
James went a journey with the goat's new compass
  And reached the end of his brick.

Ernest was an elephant and very well-intentioned,
  Leonard was a lion with a brave new tail,
George was a goat, as I think I have mentioned,
  But James was only a snail.

*A. A. Milne*

## THE GREY SQUIRREL

Like a small grey
coffee-pot,
sits the squirrel.
He is not

all he should be,
kills by dozens
trees, and eats
his red brown cousins.

The keeper, on the
other hand,
who shot him, is
a Christian, and

loves his enemies,
which shows
the squirrel was not
one of those.

*Humbert Wolfe*

# ELETELEPHONY

Once there was an elephant,
Who tried to use the telephant —
No! no! I mean an elephone
Who tried to use the telephone —
(Dear me! I am not certain quite
That even now I've got it right.)

Howe'er it was, he got his trunk
Entangled in the telephunk;
The more he tried to get it free,
The louder buzzed the telephee —
(I fear I'd better drop the song
Of elephop and telephong!)

*Laura Richards*

## THE VULTURE

The vulture eats between his meals,
And that's the reason why
He very, very rarely feels
As well as you or I.

His eye is dull, his head is bald,
His neck is growing thinner.
Oh! What a lesson for us all
To only eat at dinner!

Hilaire Belloc

# FLYING CROOKED

The butterfly, the cabbage-white,
(His honest idiocy of flight)
Will never now, it is too late,
Master the art of flying straight,
Yet has – who knows so well as I? –
A just sense of how not to fly:
He lurches here and here by guess
And God and hope and hopelessness.
Even the aerobatic swift
Has not his flying-crooked gift.

*Robert Graves*

# THERE ONCE WAS
## A PUFFIN

Oh, there once was a Puffin
Just the shape of a muffin,
And he lived on an island
In the
  bright
    blue
      sea!
He ate little fishes,
That were most delicious,
And he had them for supper
And he
  had
    them
      for tea.
But this poor little Puffin,
He couldn't play nothin',
For he hadn't anybody
To
  play
    with
      at all.
So he sat on his island,
And he cried for a while, and
He felt very lonely,
And he
  felt
    very small.

Then along came the fishes,
And they said, 'If you wishes,
You can have us for playmates,
Instead
  of
    for
      tea!'
So they now play together,
In all sorts of weather,
And the Puffin eats pancakes,
Like you
  and
    like
      me.

*Mrs F. L. Jaques*

## THE MOO-COW-MOO

The moo-cow-moo has a tail like rope,
An' it's ravelled down where it grows,
An' it's jest like feelin' a piece of soap
All over the moo-cow's nose.

The moo-cow-moo has lots of fun
Jes swingin' its tail about,
But ef he opens his mouth, I run,
Cause that's where the moo comes out.

*Edmund Vance Cook*

# THE CHRISTENING

What shall I call
    My dear little dormouse?
His eyes are small,
    But his tail is e-nor-mouse.

I sometimes call him Terrible John,
'Cos his tail goes on –
And on –
And on.
And I sometimes call him Terrible Jack,
'Cos his tail goes on to the end of his back.
And I sometimes call him Terrible James,
'Cos he says he likes me calling him names . . .

    But I think I shall call him Jim,
    'Cos I *am* fond of him.

*A. A. Milne*

# DUCKS' DITTY

All along the backwater,
Through the rushes tall,
Ducks are a-dabbling.
Up tails all!

Ducks' tails, drakes' tails,
Yellow feet a-quiver,
Yellow bills all out of sight
Busy in the river!

Slushy green undergrowth
Where the roach swim —
Here we keep our larder,
Cool and full and dim.

Every one for what he likes!
*We* like to be
Head down, tails up,
Dabbling free!

High in the blue above
Swifts whirl and call —
*We* are down a-dabbling
Up tails all!

*Kenneth Grahame*

# ON A NIGHT OF SNOW

Cat, if you go outdoors you must walk in the snow.
You will come back with little white shoes on your feet,
Little white slippers of snow that have heels of sleet.
Stay by the fire, my Cat. Lie still, do not go.
See how the flames are leaping and hissing low.
I will bring you a saucer of milk like a marguerite,
So white and so smooth, so spherical and so sweet.
Stay with me, Cat. Outdoors the wild winds blow.

Outdoors the wild winds blow, Mistress, and dark is
    the night.
Strange voices cry in the trees, intoning strange lore,
And more than cats move, lit by our eyes' green light,
On silent feet where the meadow grasses hang hoar –
Mistress, there are portents abroad of magic and
    might,
And things that are yet to be done. Open the door!

*Elizabeth Coatsworth*

# Rhymes and Riddles, Songs and Lullabies

## LIMERICKS BY EDWARD LEAR

There was an Old Man of the North,
Who fell into a basin of broth;
But a laudable cook,
Fished him out with a hook,
Which saved that Old Man of the North.

There was a Young Lady whose chin
Resembled the point of a pin:
So she had it made sharp,
And purchased a harp,
And played several tunes with her chin.

# THE RUTHLESS RHYMES OF HARRY GRAHAM

## THE STERN PARENT

Father heard his Children scream,
So he threw them in the stream,
Saying, as he drowned the third,
'Children should be seen, *not* heard!'

## NURSE'S MISTAKE

Nurse, who peppered baby's face
(She mistook it for a muffin),
Held her tongue and kept her place,
'Layin' low and sayin' nuffin' ';
Mother, seeing baby blinded,
Said, 'Oh, nurse, how absent-minded!'

# APPRECIATION

Auntie, did you feel no pain
Falling from that willow tree?
Will you do it, please, again?
'Cos my friend here didn't see.

# VERSE AND WORSE

Here lies a greedy girl, Jane Bevan,
Whose breakfasts hardly ever stopped.
One morning at half past eleven
She snapped and crackled and then popped.

*Roy Fuller*

There was an old lady of Ryde
Who ate some green apples, and died.
The apples (fermented inside the lamented)
Made cider inside 'er inside.

***Anon***

A peanut sat on the railroad track,
His heart was all a-flutter;
Along came a train – the 9.15 –
Toot, toot, peanut butter!

*Anon*

On Nevski Bridge a Russian stood
Chewing his beard for lack of food.
Said he, 'It's tough this stuff to eat
But a darn sight better than shredded wheat!'

*Anon*

Sir Christopher Wren
Said, 'I am going to dine with some men.
If anybody calls
Say I am designing St Paul's.'

*E. C. Bentley*

The rain it raineth on the just
And also on the unjust fella.
But chiefly on the just, because
The unjust steals the just's umbrella.

*Baron Charles Bowen*

# SOME ANONYMOUS LIMERICKS

There was a young lady of Lynn,
Who was so uncommonly thin
That when she essayed
To drink lemonade,
She slipped through the straw and fell in.

There was a young farmer of Leeds,
Who swallowed six packets of seeds.
It soon came to pass
He was covered with grass,
And he couldn't sit down for the weeds.

There was a young man of Bengal
Who went to a fancy-dress ball,
He went, just for fun,
Dressed up as a bun,
And a dog ate him up in the hall.

# RIDDLE-ME-REES

What's in the church
But not the steeple?
The parson has it,
But not the people.

Little Nancy Etticoat
In a white petticoat
And a red rose.
The longer she stands,
The shorter she grows.

In marble walls as white as milk,
Lined with a skin as soft as silk,
Within a fountain crystal clear,
A golden apple doth appear.
No doors there are to this stronghold.
Yet things break in and steal the gold.

As I was going to St Ives,
I met a man with seven wives;
Every wife had seven sacks;
Every sack had seven cats;
Every cat had seven kits.
Kits, cats, sacks, and wives –
How many were going to St Ives?

*Answers:*

*The letter 'r'        A Candle        An Egg
One. The others were coming from St Ives*

When I was taken from the fair body,
They then cut off my head,
And thus my shape was altered;
It's I that make peace between king and king,
And many a true lover glad:
All this I do and then times more,
And more I could do still,
But nothing can I do,
Without my guider's will.

Four stiff-standies,
Four dilly-dandies,
Two hookers,
Two snookers,
And a fling-by.

*Answers:*
A Pen     A Cow

# TRADITIONAL VERSES

## THE TRAGICAL DEATH OF
## A APPLE-PYE

A apple-pye, B bit it,
C cut it, D dealt it,
E eat it, F fought for it,
G got it, H halv'd it,
I ey'd it, J join'd for it,
M mourn'd for it, N nodded at it,
O open'd it, P peep'd in it,
Q quarter'd it, R ran for it,
S stole it, T took it,
U hew'd it, V view'd it, W wanted it;
XYZ and Ampersy-and,
They all wish'd for a piece in hand.

At last they every one agreed
Upon the apple-pye to feed;
But as there seem'd to be so many,
Those who were last might not have any,
Unless some method there was taken,
That every one might save their bacon,
They all agreed to stand in order
Around the apple-pye's fine border,
Take turn as they in hornbook stand,
From great A down to &,
In equal parts the pye divide,
As you may see on t'other side.

43

## BIRTH DAYS

Monday's child is fair of face,
Tuesday's child is full of grace,
Wednesday's child is full of woe,
Thursday's child has far to go,
Friday's child is loving and giving,
Saturday's child works hard for his living,
And the child that is born on the Sabbath day
Is bonny and blithe, and good and gay.

# SNEEZING

Sneeze on Monday, sneeze for danger;
Sneeze on Tuesday, kiss a stranger;
Sneeze on Wednesday, get a letter;
Sneeze on Thursday, something better;
Sneeze on Friday, sneeze for sorrow;
Sneeze on Saturday, see your sweetheart
    tomorrow.

## WALKING

Walk fast in snow, in frost walk slow,
And still as you go tread on your toe;
When frost and snow are both together,
Sit by the fire, and spare shoe leather.

# THE BELLS OF LONDON

Gay go up and gay go down,
To ring the bells of London Town.

Bull's eyes and targets,
Say the bells of St Margaret's.

Brickbats and tiles,
Say the bells of St Giles'.

Halfpence and farthings,
Say the bells of St Martin's.

Oranges and lemons,
Say the bells of St Clement's.

Pancakes and fritters,
Say the bells of St Peter's.

Two sticks and an apple,
Say the bells at Whitechapel.

Old Father Baldpate,
Say the slow bells at Aldgate.

Pokers and tongs,
Say the bells of St John's.

Kettles and pans,
Sav the bells of St Anne's.

You owe me ten shillings,
Say the bells of St Helen's.

When will you pay me?
Say the bells at Old Bailey.

When I grow rich,
Say the bells at Shoreditch.

Pray when will that be?
Say the bells of Stepney.

I am sure I don't know,
Says the great bell at Bow.

Here comes the candle to light
    you to bed,
And here comes the chopper
    to chop off your head.

## CHINESE SANDMEN

Chinese Sandmen,
Wise and creepy,
Croon dream-songs
To make us sleepy.
A Chinese maid with slanting eyes
Is queen of all their lullabies.
On her ancient moon-guitar
She strums a sleep-song to a star;
And when big China-shadows fall
Snow-white lilies hear her call.
Chinese Sandmen,
Wise and creepy,
Croon dream-songs
To make us sleepy.

*Anon*

# SAINT CHRISTOPHER

'Carry me, Ferryman, over the ford.'
'My boat is my back, little boy. Come aboard.
Some men have muscle, and some men have mind,
And my strength is my gift for the good of mankind.'

'Shall I not weigh on you crossing the ford?'
'I've carried a king with his crown and his sword,
A labourer too with his spade and his plough.
What's a mere child to me? Come along now.'

'Ferryman, why do you pant at the ford?'
'My muscles are iron, my sinews are cord,
But my back with your burden is ready to break,
You double your weight, child, with each step I take!'

'Ferryman, bearer of men o'er the ford,
Christopher, Christopher, I am your Lord.
My frame may be little, and slender my girth,
But they hold all the sorrows and sins of the earth.

'You have borne the whole world on your back
      through the ford,
You have carried a King with His crown and His sword,
A Labourer too with His spade and His plough,
And in one Child all little ones. Put me down now.'

Christopher set the Child down on the sward,
Christopher fell on his face by the ford.
He heard a voice uttering 'Keep me in mind!
Our strength is our gift for the good of mankind.'

*Eleanor Farjeon*

# LITTLE TREE

little tree
little silent Christmas tree
you are so little
you are more like a flower

who found you in the green forest
and were you very sorry to come away?
see   i will comfort you
because you smell so sweetly

i will kiss your cool bark
and hug you safe and tight
just as your mother would,
only don't be afraid

look   the spangles
that sleep all the year in a dark box
dreaming of being taken out and allowed to shine,
the balls the chains red and gold the fluffy threads,

put up your little arms
and i'll give them all to you to hold
every finger shall have its ring
and there won't be a single place dark or unhappy

then when you're quite dressed
you'll stand in the window for everyone to see
and how they'll stare!
oh but you'll be very proud

and my little sister and i will take hands
and looking up at our beautiful tree
we'll dance and sing
'Noel Noel'

e e cummings

## THE MOCKING BIRD SONG

Hush, little baby, don't say a word,
Papa's going to buy you a mocking bird.

If the mocking bird won't sing,
Papa's going to buy you a diamond ring.

If the diamond ring turns to brass,
Papa's going to buy you a looking-glass.

If the looking-glass gets broke,
Papa's going to buy you a billy-goat.

If that billy-goat runs away,
Papa's going to buy you another today.

Traditional American

# Girls, Boys and Peculiar People

## GRISELDA

Griselda is greedy, I'm sorry to say.
She isn't contented with four meals a day,
Like breakfast and dinner and supper and tea
(I've had to put tea after supper – you see
            *Why* don't you?)
Griselda is greedy as greedy can be.

She snoops about the larder
For sundry small supplies,
She breaks the little crusty bits
Off rims of apple pies,
She pokes the roast-potato-dish
When Sunday dinner's done,
And if there are two left in it
Griselda snitches one;
Cold chicken and cold cauliflower
She pulls in little chunks –
And when Cook calls:
            '*What* are you doing there?'
                Griselda bunks.

Griselda is greedy. Well, that's how she feels,
She simply can't help eating in-between meals,
And always forgets what it's leading to, though
The Doctor has frequently told her: 'You know
              *Why*, don't you?'
When the stomach-ache starts and Griselda says:
        'Oh.'

She slips down to the dining-room
When everyone's in bed,
For cheese-rind on the supper-tray,
And buttered crusts of bread,
A biscuit from the biscuit-box,
Lump sugar from the bowl,
A gherkin from the pickle-jar,
Are all Griselda's toll;
She tastes the salted almonds,
And she tries the candied fruits –
And when Dad shouts:
        '*Who* is it down below?'
            Griselda scoots.

Griselda is greedy. Her relatives scold,
And tell her how sorry she'll be when she's old,
She will lose her complexion, she's sure to grow fat,
She will spoil her inside – does she know what she's
    at? –
            (*Why* do they?)
*Some* people *are* greedy. Leave it at that.

*Eleanor Farjeon*

## LITTLE CLOTILDA

Little Clotilda,
Well and hearty,
Thought she'd like
To give a party.
But as her friends
Were shy and wary,
Nobody came
But her own canary.

*Anon*

# BRINGING UP BABIES

If babies could speak they'd tell mother or nurse
That slapping was pointless, and why:
For if you're not crying it prompts you to cry,
And if you are – then you cry worse.

*Roy Fuller*

## IF NO-ONE EVER MARRIES ME

If no-one ever marries me –
And I don't see why they should;
For nurse says I'm not pretty,
And I'm seldom very good –

If no-one ever marries me
I shan't mind very much;
I shall buy a squirrel in a cage,
And a little rabbit hutch.

I shall have a cottage near a wood,
And a pony all my own.
And a little lamb quite clean and tame
That I can take to town.

And when I'm getting really old,
At twenty-eight or nine,
I shall buy a little orphan girl
And bring her up as mine.

*Laurence Alma-Tadema*

# THE STORY OF AUGUSTUS

Augustus was a chubby lad;
Fat ruddy cheeks Augustus had;
And everybody saw with joy
The plump and hearty healthy boy.
He ate and drank as he was told,
And never let his soup get cold.
But one day, one cold winter's day,
He scream'd out – 'Take the soup away!
O take the nasty soup away!
I won't have any soup today.'

Next day, now, the picture shows
How lank and lean Augustus grows!
Yet, though he feels so weak and ill,
The naughty fellow cries out still –

'Not any soup for me, I say:
O take the nasty soup away!
I won't have any soup today.'

The third day comes: Oh what a sin!
To make himself so pale and thin.
Yet, when the soup is put on table,
He screams, as loud as he is able, —
'Not any soup for me, I say:
O take the nasty soup away!
I won't have any soup today.'

Look at him, now the fourth day's come!
He scarcely weighs a sugar-plum;
He's like a little bit of thread,
And on the fifth day, he was – dead!

*Dr Heinrich Hoffmann*

### CAREER

I'd rather drive an engine than
Be a little gentleman;
I'd rather go shunting and hooting
Than hunting and shooting.

*Daniel Pettiward*

## MICHAEL FINNEGAN

There once was a man called Michael Finnegan,
He grew whiskers on his chinnegan.
The wind came out and blew them in again,
Poor old Michael Finnegan! Begin again . . .

*Anon*

# 'BIBY'S' EPITAPH

A muvver was barfin' 'er biby one night,
The youngest of ten and a tiny young mite,
The muvver was poor and the biby was thin,
Only a skelington covered in skin:
The muvver turned rahnd for the soap off the rack,
She was but a moment, but when she turned back,
The biby was gorn; and in anguish she cried,
'Oh, where is my biby?' – The angels replied:

'Your biby 'as fell dahn the plug-'ole,
Your biby 'as gorn dahn the plug;
The poor little thing was so skinny and thin
'E oughter been barfed in a jug;
Your biby is perfeckly 'appy,
'E won't need a barf any more,
Your biby 'as fell dahn the plug-'ole,
Not lorst, but gorn before.'

*Anon*

# MEDITATIO

When I carefully consider the curious habits of dogs
I am compelled to conclude
That man is the superior animal.

When I consider the curious habits of man
I confess, my friend, I am puzzled.

*Ezra Pound*

# JIM

There was a Boy whose name was Jim;
His Friends were very good to him.
They gave him Tea, and Cakes, and Jam,
And slices of delicious Ham,
And Chocolate with pink inside,
And little Tricycles to ride,
And read him Stories through and through,
And even took him to the Zoo –
And there it was the dreadful Fate
Befell him, which I now relate.

You know – at least you *ought* to know,
For I have often told you so –
That Children never are allowed
To leave their Nurses in a Crowd;
Now this was Jim's especial Foible,
He ran away when he was able,
And on this inauspicious day
He slipped his hand and ran away!
He hadn't gone a yard when –
Bang!

With open Jaws a Lion sprang,
And hungrily began to eat
The Boy, beginning at his feet.
Now just imagine how it feels
When first your toes and then your heels,
And then by gradual degrees,
Your shins and ankles, calves and knees,
Are slowly eaten, bit by bit.

No wonder Jim detested it!
No wonder that he shouted 'Hi!'
The Honest Keeper heard his cry,
Though very fat he almost ran
To help the little gentleman.
'Ponto!' he ordered, as he came
(For Ponto was the Lion's name),
'Ponto!' he cried, with angry Frown.

'Let go, Sir! Down, Sir! Put it down!'
The Lion made a sudden Stop,
He let the Dainty Morsel drop,
And slunk reluctant to his Cage,
Snarling with Disappointed Rage.
But when he bent him over Jim
The Honest Keeper's Eyes were dim.
The Lion having reached the head,
The Miserable Boy was dead!

When Nurse informed his Parents, they
Were more Concerned than I can say: –
His Mother, as She dried her eyes,
Said, 'Well – it gives me no surprise,
He would not do as he was told!'
His Father, who was self-controlled,
Bade all the children round attend
To James's miserable end,
And always keep a-hold of Nurse
For fear of finding something worse.

*Hilaire Belloc*

## KINGS

King Canute
Sat down by the sea,
Up washed the tide
And away went he.

Good King Alfred
Cried, 'My sakes!
Not five winks,
And look at those cakes!'

Lackland John
Were a right royal Tartar
Till he made his mark
Upon *Magna Carta*:

Ink, seal, table,
On Runnymede green,
*Anno Domini*
12 – 15

       *Walter de la Mare*

## ADVICE TO CHILDREN

Caterpillars living on lettuce
Are the colour of their host:
Look out, when you're eating a salad,
For the greens that move the most.

Close your mouth tight when you're running
As when washing you shut your eyes,
Then as soap is kept from smarting
So will tonsils be from flies.

If in spite of such precautions
Anything nasty gets within,
Remember it will be thinking:
'Far worse for me than him.'

*Roy Fuller*

# NED

It's a singular thing that Ned
Can't be got out of bed.
    When the sun comes round
    He is sleeping sound
With the blankets over his head.
    They tell him to shunt,
    And he gives a grunt,
And burrows a little deeper –
    He's a trial to them
    At eight a.m.,
When Ned is a non-stop sleeper.
    Oh, the snuggly bits
    Where the pillow fits
    Into his cheek and neck!
    Oh, the beautiful heat
    Stored under the sheet
Which the breakfast-bell will wreck!
Oo, the noozly-oozly feel
He feels from head to heel,
    When to get out of bed
    Is worse to Ned
Than missing his morning meal!
                    *But*
It's a singular thing that Ned,
    After the sun is dead
    And the moon's come round,
    Is not to be found,
    And can't be got into bed!
                    *Eleanor Farjeon*

## MY SISTER LAURA

My sister Laura's bigger than me
And lifts me up quite easily.
I can't lift her, I've tried and tried:
She must have something heavy inside.
*Spike Milligan*

# IN JUST-

in Just-
spring      when the world is mud-
luscious the little
lame balloonman

whistles      far      and wee

and eddieandbill come
running from marbles and
piracies and it's
spring

when the world is puddle-wonderful

the queer
old balloonman whistles

far      and      wee
and bettyandisbel come dancing

from hop-scotch and jump-rope and

it's
spring
and
      the
            goat-footed
balloonMan      whistles
far
and
wee

*e e cummings*

## THE CAMEL'S HUMP

The Camel's hump is an ugly lump
Which well you may see at the Zoo;
But uglier yet is the hump we get
From having too little to do.

Kiddies and grown-ups too-oo-oo,
If we haven't enough to do-oo-oo,
We get the hump –
Cameelious hump –
The hump that is black and blue!

We climb out of bed with a frouzly head
And a snarly-yarly voice.
We shiver and scowl and we grunt and we growl
At our bath and our boots and our toys;

And there ought to be a corner for me
(And I know there is one for you)
When we get the hump –
Cameelious hump –
The hump that is black and blue!

The cure for this ill is not to sit still,
Or frowst with a book by the fire;
But to take a large hoe and a shovel also,
And dig till you gently perspire;

And then you will find that the sun and the wind,
And the Djinn of the garden too,
Have lifted the hump –
The horrible hump –
The hump that is black and blue!

I get it as well as you-oo-oo –
If I haven't enough to do-oo-oo!
We all get the hump –
Cameelious hump –
Kiddies and grown-ups too!

*Rudyard Kipling*

# Adventures and Journeys

## ADVENTURES OF ISABEL

Isabel met an enormous bear,
Isabel, Isabel, didn't care;
The bear was hungry, the bear was ravenous,
The bear's big mouth was cruel and cavernous.
The bear said, Isabel, glad to meet you,
How do, Isabel, now I'll eat you!
Isabel, Isabel, didn't worry,
Isabel didn't scream or scurry.
She washed her hands and she straightened her hair up
Then Isabel quietly ate the bear up.

Once in a night as black as pitch
Isabel met a wicked old witch.
The witch's face was cross and wrinkled,
The witch's gums with teeth were sprinkled.
Ho ho, Isabel! the old witch crowed,
I'll turn you into an ugly toad!
Isabel, Isabel, didn't worry,
Isabel didn't scream or scurry,
She showed no rage and she showed no rancour,
But she turned the witch into milk and drank her.

Isabel met a hideous giant,
Isabel continued self-reliant.
The giant was hairy, the giant was horrid,
He had one eye in the middle of his forehead.
Good morning, Isabel, the giant said,
I'll grind your bones to make my bread.
Isabel, Isabel, didn't worry,
Isabel didn't scream or scurry.
She nibbled the zwieback that she always fed off,
And when it was gone, she cut the giant's head off.

Isabel met a troublesome doctor,
He punched and he poked till he really shocked her.
The doctor's talk was of coughs and chills
And the doctor's satchel bulged with pills.
The doctor said unto Isabel,
Swallow this, it will make you well.
Isabel, Isabel, didn't worry,
Isabel didn't scream or scurry.
She took those pills from the pill concocter,
And Isabel calmly cured the doctor.

Ogden Nash

# OGGY DOGGY

Oggy was a doggy
Who wore a red hat.
Oggy was a doggy
And he was quite fat.
Oggy was a doggy
And he liked to roam the street.
Oggy was a doggy
And he had four feet.

One day Oggy doggy
Went for a walk.
Oggy doggy met Froggy
And they stopped to talk.
Froggy told Oggy he was on his way to see
His friend called Piggy,
Who'd invited him to tea.

Froggy said 'Good-bye' to Oggy,
Wished him a 'Good day',
Oggy waved his bright red hat
And carried on his way.

He had not gone but three more steps
When suddenly he found
A little pink elephant sitting on the ground.

Oggy looked and then he saw
That Elley was a-crying.
'What's the matter, baby Elley?'
Said fat Oggy, sighing.
'I'm lost!' the little pink one cried,
Staring at his boots.
'I went a-fishing with my friends –
I only caught three newts . . .'

Oggy picked up Elley
And put him on his back,
Consoled the little creature,
And then made off up the track.
He had not gone but five more steps
When suddenly they saw
Little baby Elley's mum,
Waving at the door.

'How can I repay you?'
Cried little Elley's mum.
'Thank you very much, my friend,
For bringing home my son.
How can I make up to you
This very special deed?
You just shout my name aloud
If ever you're in need.'

Oggy thanked her kindly
And then made off up the road.
It was blowing rather chilly,
And his feet were getting cold.
'Home again at last,' he said,
Feeling rather gay.
What a clever Oggy doggy!
What a busy day!

*Little Mo*


## BAD SIR BRIAN BOTANY

Sir Brian had a battleaxe with great big knobs on;
He went among the villagers and blipped them on
    the head.
On Wednesday and on Saturday, but mostly on the
    latter day,
He called at all the cottages, and this is what he said:

'I am Sir Brian!' (ting-ling)
'I am Sir Brian!' (rat-tat)
'I am Sir Brian, as bold as a lion –
Take *that*! – and *that*! – and *that*!'

Sir Brian had a pair of boots with great big spurs on,
A fighting pair of which he was particularly fond.
On Tuesday and on Friday, just to make the street
    look tidy,
He'd collect the passing villagers and kick them in the
    pond.

'I am Sir Brian!' (sper-lash!)
'I am Sir Brian!' (sper-losh!)
'I am Sir Brian, as bold as a lion –
Is anyone else for a wash?'

Sir Brian woke one morning, and he couldn't find his
    battleaxe;
He walked into the village in his second pair of boots.
He had gone a hundred paces, when the street was full
    of faces,
And the villagers were round him with ironical
    salutes,

    'You are Sir Brian? Indeed!
    You are Sir Brian? Dear, dear!
    You are Sir Brian, as bold as a lion?
    Delighted to meet you here!'

Sir Brian went a journey, and he found a lot of duck-
    weed:
They pulled him out and dried him, and they blipped
    him on the head.
They took him by the breeches, and they hurled him
    into ditches,
And they pushed him under waterfalls, and this is
    what they said:

    'You are Sir Brian – don't laugh,
    You are Sir Brian – don't cry;
    You are Sir Brian, as bold as a lion –
    Sir Brian, the lion, good-bye!'

Sir Brian struggled home again, and chopped up his
    battleaxe,
Sir Brian took his fighting boots, and threw them in
    the fire.
He is quite a different person now he hasn't got his
    spurs on,
And he goes about the village as B. Botany, Esquire.

    'I am Sir Brian? Oh, *no*!
    I am Sir Brian? Who's he?
    I haven't got any title, I'm Botany –
    Plain Mr Botany (B).'

*A. A. Milne*

# A GOOD PLAY

We built a ship upon the stairs
All made of the back-bedroom chairs,
And filled it full of sofa pillows
To go a-sailing on the billows.

We took a saw and several nails,
And water in the nursery pails:
And Tom said, 'Let us also take
An apple and a slice of cake;'
Which was enough for Tom and me
To go a-sailing on, till tea.

We sailed along for days and days,
And had the very best of plays;
But Tom fell out and hurt his knee,
So there was no one left but me.

*Robert Louis Stevenson*

## THE UPS AND DOWNS
## OF THE ELEVATOR CAR

The elevator car in the elevator shaft,
Complained of the buzzer, complained of the draught.
It said it felt carsick as it rose and fell,
It said it had a headache from the ringing of the bell

'There is spring in the air,' sighed the elevator car.
Said the elevator man, 'You are well-off where you
    are.'
The car paid no attention but it frowned an ugly frown

                when
           up      it
        going        should
    started             be
  it                     going
And                      down.

Down flashed the signal, but up went the car.
The elevator man cried, 'You are going much too far!'
Said the elevator car, 'I'm doing no such thing.
I'm through with buzzers buzzing, I'm looking for the
    spring!'

Then the elevator man began to shout and call
And all the people came running through the hall.

The elevator man began to call and shout
'The car won't stop! Let me out! Let me out!'

On went the car past the penthouse door.
On went the car up one flight more.
On went the elevator till it came to the top.
On went the elevator, and it would not stop!

Right through the roof went the man and the car.
And nobody knows where the two of them are!
(Nobody knows but everyone cares,
Wearily, drearily climbing the stairs!)

Now on a summer evening when you see a shooting
     star
Fly through the air, perhaps it is – that elevator car!
Caroline D. Emerson

## CHAIROPLANE CHANT

If everyone had a flying machine
The size of a small armchair,
Then day after day, in the promptest way
I'd go out to take air.
I'd shift a lever and press a brake,
And buzz into the blue.
Oho, the bushels of the air I'd take,
Flying to call on you.

As I skirted a steeple and skimmed a roof,
With engine whirring loud,

I'd meet you coming for dear life, humming,
Around the rim of a cloud,
We'd dodge a swallow and duck a crow,
And you would cry, 'Whoopee!
I was going to call on you, you know –
Were you coming to call on me?'

It's rather awkward to chat, of course,
From a high-geared chairoplane,
So we'd buzz away. But the very next day
We'd meet in a sky-blue lane,
With wind in our wings, and the way all clear,
And I'd sing, 'Ho, halloo,
Were you coming to call on me? O dear,
I was going to call on you!'

*Nancy Byrd Turner*

# NIGHT MAIL

This is the night mail crossing the Border,
Bringing the cheque and the postal order,

Letters for the rich, letters for the poor,
The shop at the corner, the girl next door.

Pulling up Beattock, a steady climb:
The gradient's against her, but she's on time.

Past cotton-grass and moorland boulder,
Shovelling white steam over her shoulder.

Snorting noisily, she passes
Silent miles of wind bent grasses.

Birds turn their heads as she approaches,
Stare from bushes at her blank-faced coaches.

Sheep-dogs cannot turn her course;
They slumber on with paws across.

In the farm she passes no one wakes,
But a jug in a bedroom gently shakes.

Dawn freshens, her climb is done.
Down towards Glasgow she descends,
Towards the steam tugs yelping down a glade of
    cranes,
Towards the fields of apparatus, the furnaces
Set on the dark plain like gigantic chessmen.
All Scotland waits for her:
In dark glens, beside pale-green lochs,
Men long for her news.

III

Letters of thanks, letters from banks,
Letters of joy from girl to boy,
Receipted bills and invitations
To inspect new stock or to visit relations,
And applications for situations,
And timid lovers' declarations,
News circumstantial, news financial,
Letters with holiday snaps to enlarge in,
Letters with faces scrawled on the margin,
Letters from uncles, cousins and aunts,
Letters to Scotland from the South of France,
Letters of condolence to Highlands and Lowlands,
Written on paper of every hue,
The pink, the violet, the white and the blue,

The chatty, the catty, the boring, the adoring,
The cold and official and the heart's outpouring,
Clever, stupid, short and long,
The typed and the painted and the all spelt wrong.

IV

Thousands are still asleep,
Dreaming of terrifying monsters,
Or a friendly tea beside the band in Cranston's or
    Crawford's:
Asleep in working Glasgow, asleep in well-set Edin-
    burgh,
Asleep in granite Aberdeen,
They continue their dreams,
But shall wake soon and hope for letters,
And none will hear the postman's knock
Without a quickening of the heart.
For who can bear to feel himself forgotten?

W. H. Auden

## BEGINNING OF THE ARMADILLOES

I've never sailed the Amazon,
    I've never reached Brazil;
But the *Don* and *Magdalena*,
    They can go there when they will!

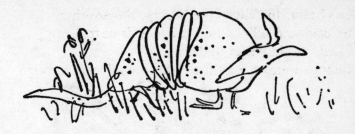

Yes, weekly from Southampton,
Great steamers, white and gold,
Go rolling down to Rio
(Roll down – roll down to Rio!)
And I'd like to roll to Rio
Some day before I'm old!

I've never seen a Jaguar,
  Nor yet an Armadill-
O dilloing in his armour,
  And I s'pose I never will,

Unless I go to Rio
These wonders to behold –
Roll down – roll down to Rio –
Roll really down to Rio!
Oh, I'd love to roll to Rio
Some day before I'm old!

*Rudyard Kipling*

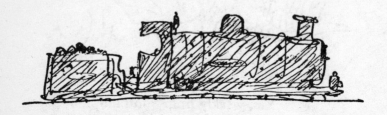

Here is the train to Glasgow.

Here is the driver,
Mr MacIver,
Who drove the train to Glasgow.

Here is the guard from Donibristle
Who waved his flag and blew his whistle
To tell the driver,
Mr MacIver,
To start the train to Glasgow.

Here is a boy called Donald MacBrain
Who came to the station to catch the train

But saw the guard from Donibristle
Wave his flag and blow his whistle
To tell the driver,
Mr MacIver
To start the train to Glasgow.

Here is the guard, a kindly man
Who, at the last moment, hauled into the van
That fortunate boy called Donald MacBrain
Who came to the station to catch the train
But saw the guard from Donibristle
Wave his flag and blow his whistle
To tell the driver,
Mr MacIver,
To start the train to Glasgow.

Here are hens and here are cocks,
Clucking and crowing inside a box,

In charge of the guard, that kindly man
Who, at the last moment, hauled into the van
That fortunate boy called Donald MacBrain
Who came to the station to catch the train
But saw the guard from Donibristle
Wave his flag and blow his whistle
To tell the driver,
Mr MacIver,
To start the train to Glasgow.

Here is the train.   It gave a jolt
Which loosened a catch and loosened a bolt,
And let out the hens and let out the cocks,
Clucking and crowing out of their box,
In charge of the guard, that kindly man
Who, at the last moment, hauled into the van
That fortunate boy called Donald MacBrain
Who came to the station to catch the train
But saw the guard from Donibristle
Wave his flag and blow his whistle
To tell the driver,
Mr MacIver,
To start the train to Glasgow.

93

The guard chased a hen and, missing it, fell.
The hens were all squawking, the cocks were as well,
And unless you were there you haven't a notion
The flurry, the fuss, the noise and commotion
Caused by the train which gave a jolt
And loosened a catch and loosened a bolt
And let out the hens and let out the cocks,
Clucking and crowing out of their box,
In charge of the guard, that kindly man
Who, at the last moment, hauled into the van
That fortunate boy called Donald MacBrain
Who came to the station to catch the train
But saw the guard from Donibristle
Wave his flag and blow his whistle
To tell the driver,
Mr MacIver,
To start the train to Glasgow.


Now Donald was quick and Donald was neat
And Donald was nimble on his feet.
He caught the hens and he caught the cocks
And he put them back in their great big box.
The guard was pleased as pleased could be
And invited Donald to come to tea

On Saturday, at Donibristle,
And let him blow his lovely whistle,
And said in all his life he'd never
Seen a boy so quick and clever,
And so did the driver,
Mr MacIver,
Who drove the train to Glasgow.

*Wilma Horsbrugh*

# ACKNOWLEDGEMENTS

The Editor gratefully acknowledges permission to reprint copyright material to the following: Edward Arnold (Publishers) Ltd. for 'The Stern Parent', 'Nurse's Mistake', and 'Appreciation' by Harry Graham, from *Ruthless Rhymes*; Mrs George Bambridge and the Macmillan Company of London and Basingstoke for 'The Beginning of the Armadilloes' and 'How the Camel Got His Hump' by Rudyard Kipling, from *The Just So Stories*; The Bodleian Library, Oxford, and Methuen & Co. Ltd., the publishers, for 'Ducks' Ditty' by Kenneth Grahame, from *The Wind in the Willows*; Andre Deutsch for 'Here lies a greedy girl, Jane Bevan', 'Bringing up Babies', and 'Advice to Children' by Roy Fuller, from *Have You Seen Grandpa Lately?*; Dennis Dobson Publishers for 'My Sister Laura', from *Silly Verse for Kids*, and 'Ant and Eleph-Ant', from *A Book of Milligananimals*, both by Spike Milligan; Gerald Duckworth & Co. Ltd. for 'Jim' and 'The Vulture' by Hilaire Belloc, from *Cautionary Verses*; Geoffrey Dearmer for his poem 'The Song of the Whale'; Faber & Faber Ltd. for 'Night Mail' by W. H. Auden, from *Collected Shorter Poems 1927-1957*, 'Skimbleshanks: The Railway Cat' by T. S. Eliot, from *Old Possum's Book of Practical Cats*, and 'Meditatio' by Ezra Pound, from *Collected Shorter Poems*; Robert Graves for his poem 'Flying Crooked', from *Collected Poems 1965*; Harcourt, Brace, Jovanovich, Inc., the publishers, for 'Chairoplane Chant' by Nancy Byrd Turner, from *Magpie Lane* by Nancy Byrd Turner, copyright 1927 by Harcourt, Brace, Jovanovich Inc., renewed 1955 by Nancy Byrd Turner; Rupert Hart-Davis for 'A Good Play' by Robert Louis Sevenson, from *The Collected Poems of R. L. Stevenson*, edited by Janet Adam-Smith; The Literary Trustees of Walter de la Mare and the Society of Authors as their representative for 'Kings' by Walter de la Mare; Little, Brown & Co. for 'Eletelephony' by Laura E. Richards, from *Tirra Lirra*; MacGibbon & Kee for 'little tree' by e e cummings and 'in Just-' by e e cummings, from *Complete Poems, Volume 1*; Mr. C. R. Milne and Methuen & Co. Ltd., the publishers, for 'The Christening', 'The Four Friends', and 'Bad Sir Brian Botany' by A. A. Milne, from *When We Were Very Young*; Methuen & Co. Ltd., the publishers, for 'The Train to Glasgow' by Wilma Horsbrugh, from *Clinkerdump*; The Estate of Ogden Nash and J. M. Dent, the publishers, for 'An Introduction to Dogs', from *Family Reunion*, and 'Adventures of Isabel', from *Parents Keep Out*; Little Mo for her poem 'Oggy Doggy'; the Oxford University Press for 'Griselda', 'Ned', and 'St. Christopher' by Eleanor Farjeon from *The Children's Bells*; Punch for 'Career' by Daniel Pettiward; William Jay Smith for his poem 'Seal', copyright William Jay Smith 1957; Miss Ann Wolfe for 'The Grey Squirrel' by Humbert Wolfe; Macmillan Publishing Company for 'On a Night of Snow' from *Night and the Cat* by Elizabeth Coatsworth; Nicholas Bentley for 'Clerihews' by E. C. Bentley.

Every effort has been made to trace the owners of the copyright material in this book. It is the Editor's belief that all necessary permissions have been obtained, but in the case of any question arising as to the use of any material, the Editor will be pleased to make the necessary correction in future editions of the book.